COUNTRIES IN THE NEWS

CANADA

Kieran Walsh

Rourke

Publishing LLC

Vero Beach, Florida 32964

www.rourkepublishing.com

The country's flag is correct at the time of going to press.

PHOTO CREDITS: ©Elsa/Getty Images pg 15; ©Corbis pgs 8, 21; ©PhotoDisc pgs 5, 6,7; All other images ©Peter Langer Associated Media Group

Title page: *Mountain sheep cross the road in Banff National Park.*

Editor: Frank Sloan

Cover and interior design by Nicola Stratford

Library of Congress Cataloging-in-Publication Data

Walsh, Kieran.
  Canada / Kieran Walsh.
     p. cm. -- (Countries in the news II)
  Includes bibliographical references and index.
  ISBN 1-59515-171-0
  1. Canada--Juvenile literature. I. Title. II. Series: Walsh, Kieran. Countries in the news II.
  F1008.2.W28 2004
  971--dc22
                                    2004009681

Printed in the USA
CG/CG

TABLE OF CONTENTS

WELCOME TO
CANADA

Canada is the largest country in land size in the western hemisphere. Canada is so big, in fact, that the country has six time zones. Just for comparison, the United States has four.

Cycling in the coastal mountains of British Columbia

Canada makes up about 40 percent of the North American **continent**. The landscape of Canada includes lowlands around the Canadian Shield (a rocky area surrounding the Hudson Bay) and mountain ranges like the Rockies. To the far north is a series of more than 50 islands called the Arctic **Archipelago**.

The Rockies begin in New Mexico and stretch through western Canada and on to Alaska.

Canada is a large country and much of the land remains untouched. This is why Canada is famous for its **wildlife**, including grizzly bears and caribou. At one time, beavers were hunted for their **pelts**. In fact, the fur trade is a large part of how Canada became a modern, **industrialized** country.

The beaver is perhaps Canada's most famous animal.

A giant Canadian grizzly bear

Moose that can grow up to 7 feet (2.1 m) tall are often seen in Canada.

THE PEOPLE

The population of Canada is more than 30 million. However, that is not a big number for such a large country. Most Canadians (around 75 percent) live in large cities close to the border with the United States—cities like Toronto, Montreal, Ottawa—Canada's capital—and Vancouver.

Toronto, Canada's largest city, is on the north shore of Lake Ontario.

Joggers enjoy Stanley Park in Vancouver.

Roughly 40 percent of Canadians are of British **ancestry**, 27 percent are of French ancestry, and another 20 percent come from other European backgrounds. The remaining population is mostly **immigrants**, many of whom have come from Asia.

About 45 percent of Canadians are Roman Catholic, and another 40 percent are Protestant. Meanwhile, about 12 percent of the population belongs to the United Church of Canada.

Canadians have access to the same kinds of **technology** that people in the United States do. Telephones, fax machines, and computers are especially important for Canadians who live in **remote** areas like the Northwest Territories.

Fishing is one of British Columbia's chief activities.

LIFE IN
CANADA

If you were to visit Canada you would find that daily life there is pretty much the same as it is in the United States. The biggest difference is in the weather.

It's always wise to bundle up in Canada's frigid winter.

Canada is a cold country—summers there can be hot, but the average temperature for the month of January is 0° F (-17° C.). Naturally, Canada also receives a lot of snow, which is why it has often been referred to as "the Great White North."

The mounted police are a common site in Canada.

The Royal Canadian Mounted Police look very different from American policemen. The *Mounties* wear red uniforms and ride horses.

SCHOOL AND SPORTS

Most Canadian children attend kindergarten for one year and move on to an eight-grade elementary school. After this, they attend a four-year secondary school. Most children who finish secondary school (about 70 percent) continue their studies at a university.

It should come as no surprise that the most popular sport in the country is ice hockey. Hockey, in fact, was invented in Canada sometime in the late 1800s. Naturally, many of the best hockey players of all time, including Wayne Gretzky and Mark Messier, hail from Canada.

The **literacy** rate in Canada is 97 percent—exactly the same as the United States.

*Mark Messier (right) is a well-known
Canadian hockey player.*

FOOD AND HOLIDAYS

Canada's history has many close ties with France, Great Britain, and now, the United States. Its food and holidays reflect the **influence** of all these countries.

For instance, Canadians enjoy tea, a beverage often associated with Britain. Pancakes with maple syrup are another favorite for cold winter days. Canadians also eat a lot of fish, particularly smoked salmon.

You can always buy delicious food at a street fair, such as this one in Quebec.

Holidays in Canada include Bastille Day, the French holiday that **commemorates** the storming of the Bastille prison every July 14th. Canadians celebrate Christmas, and they also celebrate Boxing Day on December 26th, a holiday of British origin.

THE FUTURE

Along with Mexico, Canada is one of the closest foreign countries to the United States. You can even drive there! Along with the fact that it is a beautiful country, this makes Canada a popular destination for many American **tourists**.

Several of the world's most popular entertainers are in fact Canadian. People like

A logging truck seen against the Canadian Rockies

There is much beautiful scenery in Canada, as this shot of Moraine Lake in Alberta shows.

Jim Carrey, Celine Dion, and Mike Myers were all born in Canada and later moved to the United States.

Canada will be a powerful, if subtle, force on the world for many years to come.

FAST FACTS

Area: 3,851,788 square miles (9,975,361 sq km)

Borders: Much of Canada is bordered by the waters of several oceans, including the Atlantic in the East, the Pacific in the West, and the Arctic Ocean to the North. Canada also comes into contact with large portions of the United States, both to the south and in the northwest where Alaska is located

Population: 32,207,113
Monetary Unit: Canadian dollar

Largest Cities: Toronto, Montreal, Vancouver, Calgary, Edmonton, Quebec
Government: Federation

Religions: Roman Catholic, United Church, Anglican
Crops: Wheat, barley, oilseed, tobacco, fruits, vegetables

Natural Resources: Iron ore, nickel, zinc, copper, gold, lead, molybdenum, potash, silver, fish, timber, wildlife, coal, petroleum
Major Industries: Transportation equipment, chemicals, processed and unprocessed minerals, food products, wood and paper products, fish products, petroleum, and natural gas

THE PROVINCE OF QUEBEC

Quebec is one of the easternmost of Canada's ten **provinces**, located just above the American states of New York, New Hampshire, Vermont, and Maine.

Nowhere in Canada is the French influence felt more strongly than in Quebec. The original name for Quebec was New France, and since 1974 French has been the official language of the province.

Because of these differences in language and culture, Quebec has in the past tried to **secede** from the rest of Canada. The Canadian Supreme Court has always stopped these efforts.

Montreal is Canada's second largest city.

GLOSSARY

ancestry (AN sess tree) — a person's family history

archipelago (AR kuh pel uh GO) — a group of islands

commemorates (kuh MEM uh rayts) — celebrates, remembers

continent (KONT uhn ent) — a large land mass

immigrants (IM uh grantz) — people who move from one country to another

industrialized (in DUHS tree uh lized) — based on work using machinery

influence (IN floo ents) — a powerful force

literacy (LIT ur uh see) — the ability to read and write

pelts (PELTZ) — animal skins

provinces (PRAV in cez) — divisions of a country's land

remote (ree MOTE) — far away

secede (sih SEED) — separate from

technology (teck NOL uh jee) — the use of science; machines used to make life easier

tourists (TUR ists) — people who travel

wildlife (WHY uld lyfe) — animals that don't have regular contact with humans

FURTHER READING

Find out more about Canada with these helpful books:

- Bramwell, Martyn. *The World in Maps: North America and the Caribbean.* Lerner Publications, 2000
- Braun, Eric. *Visual Geography: Canada in Pictures.* Lerner Publications, 2003
- Desaulniers, Kristi L. *Canada (Modern World Nations).* Chelsea House, 2003
- Little, Catherine and D'Arcy Little. *The Changing Face of Canada.* Raintree/Steck Vaughn, 2002
- Park, Ted. *Taking Your Camera to Canada.* Steadwell Books, 2000

WEBSITES TO VISIT

- www.infoplease.com/ipa/A0107386.html
  Infoplease – Canada
- canadaonline.about.com/index.htm?terms=canada
  About.com – Canada
- www.canadianembassy.org/homepage/index-en.asp
  Canadian Embassy – Washington, D.C.

INDEX

About the Author

Kieran Walsh is a writer of children's nonfiction books, primarily on historical and social studies topics. Walsh has been involved in the children's book field as editor, proofreader, and illustrator as well as author.

A plane on floats in rural British Columbia